DEC. 2011

Test Results for Forensic Media Preparation Tool: dc3dd: Version 7.0.0

NCJ 236225

John Laub
Director, National Institute of Justice

This report was prepared for the National Institute of Justice, U.S. Department of Justice, by the Office of Law Enforcement Standards of the National Institute of Standards and Technology under Interagency Agreement 2003–IJ–R–029.

The National Institute of Justice is a component of the Office of Justice Programs, which also includes the Bureau of Justice Assistance, the Bureau of Justice Statistics, the Office of Juvenile Justice and Delinquency Prevention, and the Office for Victims of Crime.

July 2011

Test Results for Forensic Media Preparation Tool:
dc3dd: Version 7.0.0

National Institute of
Standards and Technology
U.S. Department of Commerce

Contents

Introduction

The Computer Forensics Tool Testing (CFTT) program is a joint project of the National Institute of Justice (NIJ), the Department of Homeland Security, and the National Institute of Standards and Technology's Law Enforcement Standards Office and Information Technology Laboratory. CFTT is supported by other organizations, including the Federal Bureau of Investigation, the U.S. Department of Defense Cyber Crime Center, the U.S. Internal Revenue Service Criminal Investigation Division Electronic Crimes Program, and the U.S. Department of Homeland Security's Bureau of Immigration and Customs Enforcement, U.S. Customs and Border Protection and U.S. Secret Service. The objective of the CFTT program is to provide measurable assurance to practitioners, researchers and other applicable users that the tools used in computer forensics investigations provide accurate results. Accomplishing this requires the development of specifications and test methods for computer forensics tools and subsequent testing of specific tools against those specifications.

Test results provide the information necessary for developers to improve tools, users to make informed choices, and the legal community and others to understand the tools' capabilities. The CFTT approach to testing computer forensic tools is based on well-recognized methodologies for conformance and quality testing. The specifications and test methods are posted on the CFTT Web site (http://www.cftt.nist.gov/) for review and comment by the computer forensics community.

This document reports the results from testing the wipe function of dc3dd version 7.0.0 against the *Forensic Media Preparation Tool Test Assertions and Test Plan Version 1.0*, available at the CFTT Web site (http://www.cftt.nist.gov/fmp-atp-pc-01.pdf).

Test results for other devices and software packages using the CFTT tool methodology can be found on NIJ's CFTT Web page, http://www.nij.gov/nij/topics/forensics/evidence/digital/standards/cftt.htm.

How to Read This Report

This report is divided into four sections. The first section is a summary of the results from the test runs and is sufficient for most readers to assess the suitability of the tool for the intended use. The remaining sections of the report describe how the tests were conducted and provide documentation of test case details that support the report summary. Section 2 gives the selection of each test case from the set of possible cases defined in the test plan for forensic media preparation tools. The test cases are selected, in general, based on features offered by the tool. Section 3 lists hardware and software used to run the test cases with links to additional information about the items used. Section 4 contains a description of each test case listing all test assertions that apply, their expected results and the actual result. Please refer to the vendor's owner manual for guidance on using the tool.

Test Results for Forensic Media Preparation Tool

Tool Tested: dc3dd
Version: 7.0.0

Run Environments: DCITA LIVE Linux Ubuntu v10.04 LTS

Supplier: Department of Defense Cyber Crime Center

Tel: (410) 981-1181
                    (410) 981-1037
Toll Free: (877) 981-3235
WWW: http://www.dc3.mil/dc3/dc3About.php

1   Results Summary

The dc3dd tool can be used for a variety of forensic tasks (e.g., disk imaging or wiping media for reuse). This report only examines using the tool to overwrite media for reuse.

In all the test cases run against dc3dd version 7.0.0, all visible sectors were successfully overwritten. Sectors hidden by an HPA (FMP-03-HPA and FMP-03-DCO-HPA) were also overwritten; however, sectors hidden by a DCO were not removed (FMP-03-DCO and FMP-03-DCO-HPA). By design, the tool does not remove either Host Protected Areas (HPAs) or DCOs. However, the Linux test environment used automatically removed the HPA on test drives, allowing sectors hidden by an HPA to be overwritten by the tool.

Table 1 provides a quick overview of the test case results.

Table 1. Overview of Test Results

Test Case	Total Sectors	First Sector Overwritten	Last Sector Overwritten	Unchanged Sectors First	Unchanged Sectors Last
FMP-01-ATA28	156301488	0	156301487		
FMP-01-ATA48	488397168	0	488397167		
FMP-01-FW	488397168	0	488397167		
FMP-01-SATA28	78140160	0	78140159		
FMP-01-SATA48	312581808	0	312581807		
FMP-01-SCSI	71721820	0	71721819		
FMP-01-USB	488397168	0	488397167		
FMP-03-DCO	490234752	0	480234751	480234752	490234751
FMP-03-DCO-HPA	234441648	0	224441647	224441648	234441647
FMP-03-HPA	312581808	0	312581807		

2   Test Case Selection

The dc3dd tool was only tested for its ability to overwrite sectors of a disk drive. The overwrite command can be run in either 'wipe' or 'vwipe' modes. It supports additional options of which 'pat', 'tpat', and 'hash' (md5, sha1) were selected and varied during testing. See the 'Log Highlights' box of the Test Details, section 4.2, for more details as to the construction of each individual test setup.

The test cases were selected from cases defined by *Forensic Media Preparation Tool Test Assertions and Test Plan Version 1.0* based on features supported by this tool.

Table 2 shows which wipe modes were selected in testing.

Table 2. Selected Wipe Modes

Test Case	Mode
FMP-01-ATA28	vwipe
FMP-01-ATA48	wipe
FMP-01-FW	wipe
FMP-01-SATA28	wipe
FMP-01-SATA48	wipe
FMP-01-SCSI	wipe
FMP-01-USB	vwipe
FMP-03-DCO	wipe
FMP-03-DCO-HPA	wipe
FMP-03-HPA	wipe

The following source interfaces were used in testing: ATA28, ATA48, FW, SATA28, SATA48, SCSI and USB.

Test Materials

2.1 Support Software

Several programs were used in the setup and analysis of the test drives. These include **hdat2** (download from http://www.hdat2.com/download.html), **dsumm** (download from http://www.cftt.nist.gov/), **ransum** (download from http://www.cftt.nist.gov/) and **diskwipe** from **FS-TST Release 2.0** (download from http://www.cftt.nist.gov/diskimaging/fs-tst20.zip).

The **hdat2** program is used to create, remove and document hidden areas on a drive.

The **dsumm** program analyzes the content of a hard drive. It produces a summary of disk contents in terms of counts for each byte value present on the drive. For example, if a drive can contain 10GB (19531250 sectors of 512 bytes per sector) and the drive is wiped with zero bytes, then **dsumm** reports 10,000,000,000 zero bytes. The program also prints the first sector found with printable ASCII content.

The **ransum** program examines a hard drive to identify sectors that do not contain the content written to the drive by the **diskwipe** program. The **ransum** output is a list of sector ranges classified as either *overwritten* or *unchanged*.

The **diskwipe** program initializes a hard drive with known content.

2.2 Test Drive Creation

The following steps are used to setup a test drive:
1. The drive is initially filled with known content by the **diskwipe** program from FS-TST. The **diskwipe** program writes the sector address to each sector in both C/H/S and LBA format. The remainder of the sector bytes is set to a constant fill value unique for each drive. Each sector has known unique content after the setup. The fill value is noted in the **diskwipe** tool log file.
2. The **dsumm** program analyzes the drive contents. This documents the content of the drive.
3. If the drive is intended for hidden area tests (FMP-03, FMP-04), either an HPA, a DCO or a DCO with an HPA is created.
4. The drive size after creation of a hidden area is recorded.

2.3 Test Drive Analysis

The following steps are used to analyze a test drive after it has been wiped by the tool under test:
1. The size of the drive is recorded. This determines if the tool changes the size of a hidden area.
2. Any hidden areas still remaining on the drive are removed.
3. The **dsumm** program is run to determine the final content of the drive.
4. The **ransum** program is run to classify sectors as either *overwritten* or *unchanged*.

2.4 Test Drives

Table 3 lists the hard drives used in testing. The column labeled **Test Case** identifies the test case. The fill value written by **diskwipe** to initialize the drive is reported in the column labeled **Target Fill**. The column labeled **Model** is the model of the drive as returned by the ATA IDENTIFY DEVICE command. The column labeled **Serial #** is the serial number as returned by the ATA IDENTIFY DEVICE command.

Table 3. Fill Values by Test Case

Test Case	Target Fill (hex value)	Model	Serial #
FMP-01-ATA28	0x18	FUJITSU MHW2080AT	K004T832CK3G
FMP-01-ATA48	0x29	WDC WD2500JB-00GVC0	WD-WCAL78188039
FMP-01-FW	0x2C	FireWire/USB2.0	E
FMP-01-SATA28	0x24	FUJITSU MHW2040BH	K10XT7B278AP
FMP-01-SATA48	0x16	TOSHIBA MK1649GSY	78JBT02RT
FMP-01-SCSI	0x06	ATLAS10K2-TY367L	163022042046
FMP-01-USB	0x2C	WD2500JB-00FUA0	
FMP-03-DCO	0x24	Maxtor 7Y250P0	Y63FSHTE
FMP-03-DCO-HPA	0x1C	WDC WD1200JD-00GBB0	WD-WMAES2049679
FMP-03-HPA	0x53	WDC WD1600JB-00GVC0	WD-WMAL94865344

Table 4 lists the drive configurations for hidden sector test cases. The column labeled **Test Case** identifies the test case. The column labeled **Size** is the number of visible sectors on the drive for the test case. The size of the drive including both visible and hidden sectors is reported in the column labeled **Total**. The column labeled **Hidden** is the size in sectors of the hidden area.

Table 4. Drive Configurations for Hidden Sector Tests

Test Case	Size	Total	Hidden (DCO+HPA)
FMP-03-DCO	480234752	490234752	10000000
FMP-03-DCO-HPA	209441648	234441648	25000000 (10000000+15000000)
FMP-03-HPA	297581808	312581808	15000000

Test Results

The main item of interest for interpreting the test results is determining the conformance of the tool under test with the test assertions. Conformance with each assertion tested by a given test case is evaluated by examining the **Log Highlights** box of the test report details.

2.5 Test Results Report Key

A summary of the actual test results is presented in this report. The following table presents a description of each section of the test report summary.

Heading	Description
First Line:	Test case ID, name and version of tool tested.
Case Summary:	Test case summary from *Forensic Media Preparation Tool Test Assertions and Test Plan Version 1.0.*
Assertions:	The test assertions applicable to the test case, selected from *Forensic Media Preparation Tool Test Assertions and Test Plan Version 1.0.*

Heading	Description
Tester Name:	Name or initials of person executing test procedure.
Analysis Host:	Host used to set up test drive and analyze final drive state.
Test Host:	Host computer executing the test.
Test Date:	Time and date that test was started.
Test Drive:	Drive erased by the tool under test.
Source Setup:	Report of the native drive size, the size of any hidden areas, the apparent size of the drive (as reported by an ATA IDENTIFY DEVICE command) and an analysis of initial drive contents.
Tool Settings:	Report of tool parameters set for each test run.
Log Highlights:	Report of the state of the drive after executing the tool under test, including the apparent drive size, size of hidden area and analysis of drive contents. The ASCII content of the first non-binary-zero sector is reported.
Results:	Expected and actual results for each assertion tested.
Analysis:	Whether or not the expected results were achieved.

2.6 Test Details

2.6.1 FMP-01-ATA28

Test Case FMP-01-ATA28 DC3DD Version 7.0	
Case Summary:	FMP-01. Overwrite visible sectors using WRITE commands.
Assertions:	FMP-CA-01 All visible sectors shall be overwritten with the specified benign data.
Tester Name:	csr
Analysis host:	frank
Test host:	frank
Test date:	Thu Feb 10 13:24:56 2011
Test drive:	18-LAP

Source Setup:	Initial setup size: 156301488 from total of 156301488 (with 0 hidden)
	IDE disk: Model (FUJITSU MHW2080AT) serial # (K004T832CK3G)
	
	Sector 0 is first sector with printable text
	============= Start text =============
	00000/000/01 000000000000
	============= End text Sector 0 =============
	1 <new line> character inserted for readability
	
	Totals for all sectors
	summary format: <count> <hex value> <(actual character if printable)> ...
	    156301488 00 75907021680 18 156301488 20 ( )
	    312602976 2F (/) 1092738319 30 (0) 445157427 31 (1)
	    274740905 32 (2) 274642393 33 (3) 272159917 34 (4)
	    262536293 35 (5) 225709546 36 (6) 215483146 37 (7)
	    215483143 38 (8) 215483135 39 (9)
	Totals for non-ASCII sectors
	summary format: <count> <hex value> <(actual character if printable)> ...
	
	80026361856 bytes, 156301488 sectors, 14 distinct values seen
	156301488 sectors have printable text

Tool Settings:	type: vwipe pattern: none hash: md5

Log Highlights:	======== dc3dd tool log (start) =========== dc3dd 7.0.0 started at 2011-02-10 10:17:06 -0500 compiled options: DEFAULT_HASH_MD5 (hash=md5) DEFAULT_HASH_SHA1 (hash=sha1) DEFAULT_VERBOSE_REPORTING (verb=on) command line: dc3dd vwipe=/dev/sda hash=md5 log=tool-log.txt device size: 156301488 sectors (probed) sector size: 512 bytes (probed) 80026361856 bytes (75 G) copied (100%), 5426.14 s, 14 M/s output hashing (100%) input results for pattern `00':    156301488 sectors in    1b26c0e62b79f528793199a3d2de4034 (md5)  output results for device `/dev/sda': 156301488 sectors out [ok] 1b26c0e62b79f528793199a3d2de4034 (md5) dc3dd completed at 2011-02-10 11:47:32 -0500 ======== dc3dd tool log (end) =========== hash verfiy: 1b26c0e62b79f528793199a3d2de4034 /dev/sda Size after tool runs: 156301488 from total of 156301488 (with 0 hidden) Analysis of tool result -- Totals for all sectors summary format: <count> <hex value> <(actual character if printable)> ... 80026361856 00 Totals for non-ASCII sectors summary format: <count> <hex value> <(actual character if printable)> ... 80026361856 00 80026361856 bytes, 156301488 sectors, 1 distinct values seen No sectors have printable text Runs of Sectors Unchanged or Overwritten First Sector Last Sector State 0 -- 156301487 Overwritten

Results:	**Assertion & Expected Result**	**Actual Result**	
	FMP-CA-01 Visible sectors overwritten	as expected	
Analysis:	Expected results achieved		

2.6.2 FMP-01-ATA48

Test Case FMP-01-ATA48 DC3DD Version 7.0	
Case Summary:	FMP-01. Overwrite visible sectors using WRITE commands.
Assertions:	FMP-CA-01 All visible sectors shall be overwritten with the specified benign data.
Tester Name:	csr
Analysis host:	frank
Test host:	frank
Test date:	Fri Feb 11 14:19:23 2011
Test drive:	29-IDE
Source Setup:	Initial setup size: 488397168 from total of 488397168 (with 0 hidden) IDE disk: Model (WDC WD2500JB-00GVC0) serial # (WD-WCAL78188039) Sector 0 is first sector with printable text ============= Start text ============= 00000/000/01 000000000000))))))))))))))))))))))))))):)))))))))))))):)))))))))))

```
))))))))))))))))))))))))))))))))))))))))))))))))))))))))))))))))))))))))
))))))))))))))))))))))))))))))))))))))))))))))))))))))))))))))))))))))))
))))))))))))))))))))))))))))))))))))))))))))))))))))))))))))))))))))))))
))))))))))))))))))))))))))))))))))))))))))))))))))))))))))))))))))))))))
))))))))))))))))))))))))))))))))))))))))))))))))))))))))))))))))))))))))
))))))))))))))))))))))))))))))))))))))))))))))))))))))))))))))))))))))))
)))))))))))))))))))))))))))))))))))))
============== End text Sector 0 ==============
9 <new line> characters inserted for readability

Totals for all sectors
summary format: <count> <hex value> <(actual character if printable)> ...
    488397168 00        488397168 20 ( ) 237361023648 29 ())
    976794336 2F (/)    2735169210 30 (0)   1278997882 31 (1)
   1192805876 32 (2)     933260747 33 (3)    905775911 34 (4)
    805865997 35 (5)     749775664 36 (6)    718765480 37 (7)
    716559080 38 (8)     707761849 39 (9)
Totals for non-ASCII sectors
summary format: <count> <hex value> <(actual character if printable)> ...

250059350016 bytes, 488397168 sectors, 14 distinct values seen
488397168 sectors have printable text
```

Tool Settings:	type: wipe pattern:0xb9

Log Highlights:	```======== dc3dd tool log (start) ============```
	
	```dc3dd 7.0.0 started at 2011-02-14 02:15:29 -0500```
	```compiled options: DEFAULT_HASH_MD5 (hash=md5) DEFAULT_HASH_SHA1 (hash=sha1)```
	```DEFAULT_VERBOSE_REPORTING (verb=on)```
	```command line: dc3dd wipe=/dev/sda pat=b9 log=tool-log.txt```
	```device size: 488397168 sectors (probed)```
	```sector size: 512 bytes (probed)```
	```250059350016 bytes (233 G) copied (100%), 4905.21 s, 49 M/s```
	
	```input results for pattern `b9':```
	``` 488397168 sectors in```
	``` 6bb3bf6e6d66233bc5994f3f16c61bad (md5)```
	``` aff2e2f2656002b5463f6adc34db23793760a97f (sha1)```
	
	```output results for device `/dev/sda':```
	``` 488397168 sectors out```
	
	```dc3dd completed at 2011-02-14 03:37:14 -0500```
	
	```======== dc3dd tool log (end) ============```
	```Size after tool runs: 488397168 from total of 488397168 (with 0 hidden)```
	```Analysis of tool result --```
	```Totals for all sectors```
	```summary format: <count> <hex value> <(actual character if printable)> ...```
	```250059350016 B9```
	```Totals for non-ASCII sectors```
	```summary format: <count> <hex value> <(actual character if printable)> ...```
	```250059350016 B9```
	
	```250059350016 bytes, 488397168 sectors, 1 distinct values seen```
	```No sectors have printable text```
	
	``` Runs of Sectors Unchanged or Overwritten```
	```First Sector Last Sector State```
	``` 0 -- 488397167 Overwritten```

Results:	**Assertion & Expected Result**	**Actual Result**
	FMP-CA-01 Visible sectors overwritten	as expected
Analysis:	Expected results achieved	

2.6.3 FMP-01-FW

Test Case FMP-01-FW DC3DD Version 7.0	
Case Summary:	FMP-01. Overwrite visible sectors using WRITE commands.
Assertions:	FMP-CA-01 All visible sectors shall be overwritten with the specified benign data.
Tester Name:	csr
Analysis host:	frank
Test host:	frank
Test date:	Tue Feb 22 14:26:07 2011
Test drive:	2C-FU2

Source Setup:	Initial setup size: 488397168 from total of 488397168 (with 0 hidden)
	Model (FireWire/USB2.0) serial # (E)
	
	Sector 0 is first sector with printable text
	============= Start text =============
	00000/000/01 000000000000,,,,,,,,,,,,,,,,,,,,,,,,,,,,,,,,,,,,
	,,
	,,
	,,
	,,
	,,
	,,
	,,
	,,,,,,,,,,,,,,,,,,,,,,,,,,,,,,,,,,
	============= End text Sector 0 =============
	9 <new line> characters inserted for readability
	
	Totals for all sectors
	summary format: <count> <hex value> <(actual character if printable)> ...
	   488397168 00 488397168 20 ( ) 237361023648 2C (,)
	   976794336 2F (/) 2735169210 30 (0) 1278997882 31 (1)
	  1192805876 32 (2) 933260747 33 (3) 905775911 34 (4)
	   805865997 35 (5) 749775664 36 (6) 718765480 37 (7)
	   716559080 38 (8) 707761849 39 (9)
	Totals for non-ASCII sectors
	summary format: <count> <hex value> <(actual character if printable)> ...
	
	250059350016 bytes, 488397168 sectors, 14 distinct values seen
	488397168 sectors have printable text

Tool Settings:	type: wipe pattern: 0xb9
Log Highlights:	======== dc3dd tool log (start) ============ dc3dd 7.0.0 started at 2011-02-23 02:16:33 -0500 compiled options: DEFAULT_HASH_MD5 (hash=md5) DEFAULT_HASH_SHA1 (hash=sha1) DEFAULT_VERBOSE_REPORTING (verb=on) command line: dc3dd wipe=/dev/sda pat=b9 log=tool-log.txt device size: 488397168 sectors (probed) sector size: 512 bytes (probed) 250059350016 bytes (233 G) copied (100%), 10341.3 s, 23 M/s input results for pattern `b9':   488397168 sectors in   6bb3bf6e6d66233bc5994f3f16c61bad (md5)   aff2e2f2656002b5463f6adc34db23793760a97f (sha1)  output results for device `/dev/sda':

	488397168 sectors out
	dc3dd completed at 2011-02-23 05:08:54 -0500
	======== dc3dd tool log (end) ============
	Size after tool runs: 488397168 from total of 488397168 (with 0 hidden)
	Analysis of tool result --
	Totals for all sectors
	summary format: \<count\> \<hex value\> \<(actual character if printable)\> ...
	250059350016 B9
	Totals for non-ASCII sectors
	summary format: \<count\> \<hex value\> \<(actual character if printable)\> ...
	250059350016 B9
	250059350016 bytes, 488397168 sectors, 1 distinct values seen
	No sectors have printable text
	Runs of Sectors Unchanged or Overwritten
	First Sector Last Sector State
	0 -- 488397167 Overwritten

Results:	**Assertion & Expected Result**	**Actual Result**	
	FMP-CA-01 Visible sectors overwritten	as expected	
Analysis:	Expected results achieved		

2.6.4 FMP-01-SATA28

Test Case FMP-01-SATA28 DC3DD Version 7.0	
Case Summary:	FMP-01. Overwrite visible sectors using WRITE commands.
Assertions:	FMP-CA-01 All visible sectors shall be overwritten with the specified benign data.
Tester Name:	csr
Analysis host:	frank
Test host:	frank
Test date:	Mon Feb 14 13:21:50 2011
Test drive:	24-LAP
Source Setup:	Initial setup size: 78140160 from total of 78140160 (with 0 hidden)
	IDE disk: Model (FUJITSU MHW2040BH) serial # (K10XT7B278AP)
	Sector 0 is first sector with printable text
	============= Start text =============
	00000/000/01 000000000000$$$$$$$$$$$$$$$$$$$$$$$$$$$$$$$$$$
	$$
	$$
	$$
	$$
	$$
	$$
	$$
	$$$$$$$$$$$$$$$$$$$$$$$$$$$$$$$$$$$
	============= End text Sector 0 =============
	9 \<new line\> characters inserted for readability
	Totals for all sectors
	summary format: \<count\> \<hex value\> \<(actual character if printable)\> ...
	78140160 00 78140160 20 ( ) 37976117760 24 ($)
	156280320 2F (/) 561878293 30 (0) 173598093 31 (1)
	159768433 32 (2) 142914673 33 (3) 139463608 34 (4)
	123744696 35 (5) 114674216 36 (6) 107788836 37 (7)
	98210496 38 (8) 97042176 39 (9)
	Totals for non-ASCII sectors
	summary format: \<count\> \<hex value\> \<(actual character if printable)\> ...

	40007761920 bytes, 78140160 sectors, 14 distinct values seen 78140160 sectors have printable text
Tool Settings:	type: wipe pattern: 'b9'
Log Highlights:	======== dc3dd tool log (start) ============ dc3dd 7.0.0 started at 2011-02-14 08:54:53 -0500 compiled options: DEFAULT_HASH_MD5 (hash=md5) DEFAULT_HASH_SHA1 (hash=sha1) DEFAULT_VERBOSE_REPORTING (verb=on) command line: dc3dd wipe=/dev/sda tpat=b9 log=tool-log.txt device size: 78140160 sectors (probed) sector size: 512 bytes (probed) 40007761920 bytes (37 G) copied (100%), 1081.64 s, 35 M/s input results for pattern `b9':    78140160 sectors in    cff3e9b4544a166d73fa015fee1213ff (md5)    b453900e36e88a52fde009a8a8c1cc6632c875da (sha1)  output results for device `/dev/sda': 78140160 sectors out dc3dd completed at 2011-02-14 09:12:55 -0500 ======== dc3dd tool log (end) =========== Size after tool runs: 78140160 from total of 78140160 (with 0 hidden) Analysis of tool result -- Sector 0 is first sector with printable text ============= Start text ============= b9b9b9b9b9b9b9b9b9b9b9b9b9b9b9b9b9b9b9b9b9b9b9b9b9b9b9b9b9 b9b9b9b9b9b9b9b9b9b9b9b9b9b9b9b9b9b9b9b9b9b9b9b9b9b9b9b9b9 b9b9b9b9b9b9b9b9b9b9b9b9b9b9b9b9b9b9b9b9b9b9b9b9b9b9b9b9b9 b9b9b9b9b9b9b9b9b9b9b9b9b9b9b9b9b9b9b9b9b9b9b9b9b9b9b9b9b9 b9b9b9b9b9b9b9b9b9b9b9b9b9b9b9b9b9b9b9b9b9b9b9b9b9b9b9b9b9 b9b9b9b9b9b9b9b9b9b9b9b9b9b9b9b9b9b9b9b9b9b9b9b9b9b9b9b9b9 b9b9b9b9b9b9b9b9b9b9b9b9b9b9b9b9b9b9b9b9b9b9b9b9b9b9b9b9b9 b9b9b9b9b9b9b9b9b9b9b9b9b9b9b9b9b9b9b9b9b9b9b9b9b9b9b9b9b9 b9b9b9b9b9b9b9b9b9b9b9b9b9b9b9b9b9 ============= End text Sector 0 ============= 9 <new line> characters inserted for readability Totals for all sectors summary format: <count> <hex value> <(actual character if printable)> ... 20003880960 39 (9) 20003880960 62 (b) Totals for non-ASCII sectors summary format: <count> <hex value> <(actual character if printable)> ... 40007761920 bytes, 78140160 sectors, 2 distinct values seen 78140160 sectors have printable text Runs of Sectors Unchanged or Overwritten First Sector Last Sector State 0 -- 78140159 Overwritten

Results:	**Assertion & Expected Result**	**Actual Result**	
	FMP-CA-01 Visible sectors overwritten	as expected	
Analysis:	Expected results achieved		

2.6.5 FMP-01-SATA48

Test Case FMP-01-SATA48 DC3DD Version 7.0	
Case Summary:	FMP-01. Overwrite visible sectors using WRITE commands.
Assertions:	FMP-CA-01 All visible sectors shall be overwritten with the specified benign data.
Tester Name:	csr
Analysis host:	frank
Test host:	frank
Test date:	Tue Feb 15 07:17:19 2011
Test drive:	16-LAP

Source Setup:	Initial setup size: 312581808 from total of 312581808 (with 0 hidden)
	IDE disk: Model (TOSHIBA MK1649GSY) serial # (78JBT02RT)
	
	Sector 0 is first sector with printable text
	============== Start text ==============
	00000/000/01 000000000000
	============== End text Sector 0 ==============
	1 <new line> character inserted for readability
	
	Totals for all sectors
	summary format: \<count> \<hex value> \<(actual character if printable)> ...
	   312581808 00 151914758688 16 312581808 20 ( )
	   625163616 2F (/) 1850492169 30 (0) 906528227 31 (1)
	   696435016 32 (2) 541016511 33 (3) 522787395 34 (4)
	   514450557 35 (5) 478352540 36 (6) 458495114 37 (7)
	   458481159 38 (8) 449761088 39 (9)
	Totals for non-ASCII sectors
	summary format: \<count> \<hex value> \<(actual character if printable)> ...
	
	160041885696 bytes, 312581808 sectors, 14 distinct values seen
	312581808 sectors have printable text

Tool Settings:	type: wipe pattern: 0xb9
Log Highlights:	======== dc3dd tool log (start) =========== dc3dd 7.0.0 started at 2011-02-15 04:09:47 -0500 compiled options: DEFAULT_HASH_MD5 (hash=md5) DEFAULT_HASH_SHA1 (hash=sha1) DEFAULT_VERBOSE_REPORTING (verb=on) command line: dc3dd wipe=/dev/sda pat=b9 log=tool-log.txt device size: 312581808 sectors (probed) sector size: 512 bytes (probed) 160041885696 bytes (149 G) copied (100%), 3368.32 s, 45 M/s input results for pattern `b9':    312581808 sectors in    2e6266f2e269caa7f6812432b48204fc (md5)    fb5ad4a6489416e47ca3ceb52b4d79f22d7b189c (sha1)  output results for device `/dev/sda': 312581808 sectors out dc3dd completed at 2011-02-15 05:05:55 -0500 ======== dc3dd tool log (end) =========== Size after tool runs: 312581808 from total of 312581808 (with 0 hidden) Analysis of tool result -- Totals for all sectors summary format: \<count> \<hex value> \<(actual character if printable)> ... 160041885696 B9 Totals for non-ASCII sectors summary format: \<count> \<hex value> \<(actual character if printable)> ... 160041885696 B9 160041885696 bytes, 312581808 sectors, 1 distinct values seen

Test Case FMP-01-SATA48 DC3DD Version 7.0	
	No sectors have printable text Runs of Sectors Unchanged or Overwritten First Sector Last Sector State 0 -- 312581807 Overwritten

Results:	Assertion & Expected Result	Actual Result	
	FMP-CA-01 Visible sectors overwritten	as expected	
Analysis:	Expected results achieved		

2.6.6 FMP-01-SCSI

Test Case FMP-01-SCSI DC3DD Version 7.0	
Case Summary:	FMP-01. Overwrite visible sectors using WRITE commands.
Assertions:	FMP-CA-01 All visible sectors shall be overwritten with the specified benign data.
Tester Name:	csr
Analysis host:	frank
Test host:	frank
Test date:	Thu Feb 24 13:20:21 2011
Test drive:	06

Source
Setup:
	Initial setup size: 71721820 from total of 71721820 (with 0 hidden)
	Model (ATLAS10K2-TY367L) serial # (163022042046)
	
	Sector 0 is first sector with printable text
	============= Start text =============
	00000/000/01 000000000000
	============= End text Sector 0 =============
	1 <new line> character inserted for readability
	
	Totals for all sectors
	summary format: <count> <hex value> <(actual character if printable)> ...
	   71721820 00 34856804520 06 71721820 20 ( )
	  143443640 2F (/) 519143675 30 (0) 162528133 31 (1)
	  149139936 32 (2) 133670254 33 (3) 123349540 34 (4)
	  113156848 35 (5) 104831312 36 (6) 91849268 37 (7)
	   90105547 38 (8) 90105527 39 (9)
	Totals for non-ASCII sectors
	summary format: <count> <hex value> <(actual character if printable)> ...
	
	36721571840 bytes, 71721820 sectors, 14 distinct values seen
	71721820 sectors have printable text

Tool Settings:	type: wipe pattern: 'b9'

Log
Highlights:
	======== dc3dd tool log (start) ===========
	
	dc3dd 7.0.0 started at 2011-02-24 08:58:38 -0500
	compiled options: DEFAULT_HASH_MD5 (hash=md5) DEFAULT_HASH_SHA1 (hash=sha1)
	DEFAULT_VERBOSE_REPORTING (verb=on)
	command line: dc3dd wipe=/dev/sde tpat=b9 log=tool-log.txt
	device size: 71721820 sectors (probed)
	sector size: 512 bytes (probed)
	36721571840 bytes (34 G) copied (100%), 1143.54 s, 31 M/s
	
	input results for pattern `b9':
	  71721820 sectors in
	  9e7af39aed8afc73458fcabc1d59a18b (md5)
	  2d61144c427f4b7cbd72a33cb7a045b227220bfd (sha1)

```
                output results for device `/dev/sde':
                   71721820 sectors out

                dc3dd completed at 2011-02-24 09:17:41 -0500

                ======== dc3dd tool log (end) ============
                Size after tool runs: 71721820 from total of 71721820 (with 0 hidden)
                Analysis of tool result --

                Sector 0 is first sector with printable text
                ============= Start text =============
                b9b9b9b9b9b9b9b9b9b9b9b9b9b9b9b9b9b9b9b9b9b9b9b9b9b9b9b9b9b9b9
                b9b9b9b9b9b9b9b9b9b9b9b9b9b9b9b9b9b9b9b9b9b9b9b9b9b9b9b9b9b9b9
                b9b9b9b9b9b9b9b9b9b9b9b9b9b9b9b9b9b9b9b9b9b9b9b9b9b9b9b9b9b9b9
                b9b9b9b9b9b9b9b9b9b9b9b9b9b9b9b9b9b9b9b9b9b9b9b9b9b9b9b9b9b9b9
                b9b9b9b9b9b9b9b9b9b9b9b9b9b9b9b9b9b9b9b9b9b9b9b9b9b9b9b9b9b9b9
                b9b9b9b9b9b9b9b9b9b9b9b9b9b9b9b9b9b9b9b9b9b9b9b9b9b9b9b9b9b9b9
                b9b9b9b9b9b9b9b9b9b9b9b9b9b9b9b9b9b9b9b9b9b9b9b9b9b9b9b9b9b9b9
                b9b9b9b9b9b9b9b9b9b9b9b9b9b9b9b9b9b9b9b9b9b9b9b9b9b9b9b9b9b9b9
                b9b9b9b9b9b9b9b9b9b9b9b9b9b9b9b9b9
                ============= End text Sector 0 =============
                9 <new line> characters inserted for readability

                Totals for all sectors
                summary format: <count> <hex value> <(actual character if printable)> ...
                 18360785920 39 (9)  18360785920 62 (b)
                Totals for non-ASCII sectors
                summary format: <count> <hex value> <(actual character if printable)> ...

                36721571840 bytes, 71721820 sectors, 2 distinct values seen
                71721820 sectors have printable text


                    Runs of Sectors Unchanged or Overwritten
                First Sector      Last Sector      State
                        0 --      71721819    Overwritten
```

Results:	Assertion & Expected Result	Actual Result	
	FMP-CA-01 Visible sectors overwritten	as expected	
Analysis:	Expected results achieved		

2.6.7 FMP-01-USB

Test Case FMP-01-USB DC3DD Version 7.0	
Case Summary:	FMP-01. Overwrite visible sectors using WRITE commands.
Assertions:	FMP-CA-01 All visible sectors shall be overwritten with the specified benign data.
Tester Name:	csr
Analysis host:	frank
Test host:	frank
Test date:	Wed Feb 16 15:12:25 2011
Test drive:	2C-FU2
Source Setup:	Initial setup size: 488397168 from total of 488397168 (with 0 hidden) Model (WD2500JB-00FUA0) serial # () Sector 0 is first sector with printable text ============= Start text ============= 00000/000/01 000000000000,,,,,,,,,,,,,,,,,,,,,,,,,,,,,,,,,, ,,, ,,, ,,, ,,, ,,, ,,,

```
                 ,,,,,,,,,,,,,,,,,,,,,,,,,,,,,,,,,,,,,,,,,,,,,,,,,,,,,,,,,,
                 ,,,,,,,,,,,,,,,,,,,,,,,,,,,,,,,,,
                 ============= End text Sector 0 ==============
                 9 <new line> characters inserted for readability

                 Totals for all sectors
                 summary format: <count> <hex value> <(actual character if printable)> ...
                    488397168 00        488397168 20 ( ) 237361023648 2C (,)
                    976794336 2F (/)   2735169210 30 (0)  1278997882 31 (1)
                   1192805876 32 (2)    933260747 33 (3)   905775911 34 (4)
                    805865997 35 (5)    749775664 36 (6)   718765480 37 (7)
                    716559080 38 (8)    707761849 39 (9)
                 Totals for non-ASCII sectors
                 summary format: <count> <hex value> <(actual character if printable)> ...

                 250059350016 bytes, 488397168 sectors, 14 distinct values seen
                 488397168 sectors have printable text
```

Tool Settings:	type: vwipe pattern: 'b9' hash: sha1
| Log Highlights: | ```
======== dc3dd tool log (start) ============

dc3dd 7.0.0 started at 2011-02-17 03:10:51 -0500
compiled options: DEFAULT_HASH_MD5 (hash=md5) DEFAULT_HASH_SHA1 (hash=sha1)
DEFAULT_VERBOSE_REPORTING (verb=on)
command line: dc3dd vwipe=/dev/sda tpat=b9 hash=sha1 log=tool-log.txt
device size: 488397168 sectors (probed)
sector size: 512 bytes (probed)
250059350016 bytes (233 G) copied (100%), 17943.3 s, 13 M/s
output hashing (100%)

input results for pattern `b9':
   488397168 sectors in
   c29e0af7e7f317b291e018b6c2a994d1103bc71c (sha1)

output results for device `/dev/sda':
   488397168 sectors out
   [ok] c29e0af7e7f317b291e018b6c2a994d1103bc71c (sha1)

dc3dd completed at 2011-02-17 13:09:50 -0500

======== dc3dd tool log (end) ============
hash verify: c29e0af7e7f317b291e018b6c2a994d1103bc71c  /dev/sda

Size after tool runs: 488397168 from total of 488397168 (with 0 hidden)
Analysis of tool result --

Sector 0 is first sector with printable text
============= Start text =============
b9b9b9b9b9b9b9b9b9b9b9b9b9b9b9b9b9b9b9b9b9b9b9b9b9b9b9b9b9b9b9b9
b9b9b9b9b9b9b9b9b9b9b9b9b9b9b9b9b9b9b9b9b9b9b9b9b9b9b9b9b9b9b9b9
b9b9b9b9b9b9b9b9b9b9b9b9b9b9b9b9b9b9b9b9b9b9b9b9b9b9b9b9b9b9b9b9
b9b9b9b9b9b9b9b9b9b9b9b9b9b9b9b9b9b9b9b9b9b9b9b9b9b9b9b9b9b9b9b9
b9b9b9b9b9b9b9b9b9b9b9b9b9b9b9b9b9b9b9b9b9b9b9b9b9b9b9b9b9b9b9b9
b9b9b9b9b9b9b9b9b9b9b9b9b9b9b9b9b9b9b9b9b9b9b9b9b9b9b9b9b9b9b9b9
b9b9b9b9b9b9b9b9b9b9b9b9b9b9b9b9b9b9b9b9b9b9b9b9b9b9b9b9b9b9b9b9
b9b9b9b9b9b9b9b9b9b9b9b9b9b9b9b9b9b9b9b9b9b9b9b9
============= End text Sector 0 =============
9 <new line> characters inserted for readability

Totals for all sectors
summary format: <count> <hex value> <(actual character if printable)> ...
125029675008 39 (9) 125029675008 62 (b)
Totals for non-ASCII sectors
summary format: <count> <hex value> <(actual character if printable)> ...
``` |
```

Test Case FMP-01-USB DC3DD Version 7.0	

	250059350016 bytes, 488397168 sectors, 2 distinct values seen
	488397168 sectors have printable text
	
	    Runs of Sectors Unchanged or Overwritten
	First Sector Last Sector State
	    0 -- 488397167 Overwritten

Results:	Assertion & Expected Result	Actual Result	
	FMP-CA-01 Visible sectors overwritten	as expected	
Analysis:	Expected results achieved		

2.6.8 FMP-03-DCO

Test Case FMP-03-DCO DC3DD Version 7.0	
Case Summary:	FMP-03. Overwrite hidden sectors using WRITE commands.
Assertions:	FMP-CA-01 All visible sectors shall be overwritten with the specified benign data. FMP-AO-01 If there is a hidden area present and the tool supports overwriting sectors contained in a hidden area, then all sectors contained in the hidden area shall be overwritten with the specified benign data. FMP-AO-02 A hidden area may optionally be removed from the storage device.
Tester Name:	csr
Analysis host:	frank
Test host:	frank
Test date:	Fri Feb 25 10:52:37 2011
Test drive:	2A-IDE

Source Setup:	Initial setup size: 480234752 from total of 490234752 (with 10000000 hidden)
	IDE disk: Model (Maxtor 7Y250P0) serial # (Y63FSHTE)
	
	Sector 0 is first sector with printable text
	============= Start text =============
	00000/000/01 000000000000*********************************
	***
	***
	***
	***
	***
	***
	***
	******************************
	============= End text Sector 0 =============
	9 \<new line> characters inserted for readability
	
	Totals for all sectors
	summary format: \<count> \<hex value> \<(actual character if printable)> ...
	   480234752 00 480234752 20 ( ) 233394089472 2A (*)
	   960469504 2F (/) 2688406892 30 (0) 1262709725 31 (1)
	  1176182573 32 (2) 913616218 33 (3) 886219489 34 (4)
	   794684344 35 (5) 739530848 36 (6) 709039708 37 (7)
	   699165650 38 (8) 695609097 39 (9)
	Totals for non-ASCII sectors
	summary format: \<count> \<hex value> \<(actual character if printable)> ...
	
	245880193024 bytes, 480234752 sectors, 14 distinct values seen
	480234752 sectors have printable text

Tool Settings:	type: wipe pattern: 0xb9
Log	======== dc3dd tool log (start) ===========

```
Test Case FMP-03-DCO DC3DD Version 7.0
```

Highlights:	
| | ```
dc3dd 7.0.0 started at 2011-02-25 08:11:18 -0500
compiled options: DEFAULT_HASH_MD5 (hash=md5) DEFAULT_HASH_SHA1 (hash=sha1)
DEFAULT_VERBOSE_REPORTING (verb=on)
command line: dc3dd wipe=/dev/sda pat=b9 log=tool-log.txt
device size: 480234752 sectors (probed)
sector size: 512 bytes (probed)
245880193024 bytes (229 G) copied (100%), 5030.42 s, 47 M/s

input results for pattern `b9':
   480234752 sectors in
   928402193b64b55e541655443d704f95 (md5)
   228e308df669884aa7a11eb625f7be0c8c875d50 (sha1)

output results for device `/dev/sda':
   480234752 sectors out

dc3dd completed at 2011-02-25 09:35:09 -0500

========= dc3dd tool log (end) ============
Size after tool runs: 480234752 from total of 490234752 (with 10000000
hidden)
Analysis of tool result --

Sector 480234752 is first sector with printable text
============== Start text ==============
29893/058/54 000480234752*********************************
*****************************************************
*****************************************************
*****************************************************
*****************************************************
*****************************************************
*****************************************************
*****************************************************
******************************
============== End text Sector 480234752 ==============
9 <new line> characters inserted for readability

Totals for all sectors
summary format: <count> <hex value> <(actual character if printable)> ...
   10000000 00         10000000 20 ( )    4860000000 2A (*)
   20000000 2F (/)     57509778 30 (0)      19475822 31 (1)
   19331121 32 (2)     23757753 33 (3)      25317978 34 (4)
   13723905 35 (5)     12312621 36 (6)      11677634 37 (7)
   21551073 38 (8)     15342315 39 (9) 245880193024 B9
Totals for non-ASCII sectors
summary format: <count> <hex value> <(actual character if printable)> ...
245880193024 B9

251000193024 bytes, 490234752 sectors, 15 distinct values seen
10000000 sectors have printable text


     Runs of Sectors Unchanged or Overwritten
First Sector      Last Sector      State
        0 --        480234751   Overwritten
  480234752 --      490234751   Unchanged
``` |

Results:	Assertion & Expected Result	Actual Result	
	FMP-CA-01 Visible sectors overwritten	as expected	
	FMP-AO-01 Hidden sectors overwritten	DCO not overwritten	
	FMP-AO-02 Hidden area final state is	in place	
Analysis:	Expected results not achieved		
```

2.6.9 FMP-03-DCO-HPA

Test Case FMP-03-DCO-HPA DC3DD Version 7.0	
Case Summary:	FMP-03. Overwrite hidden sectors using WRITE commands.
Assertions:	FMP-CA-01 All visible sectors shall be overwritten with the specified benign data. FMP-AO-01 If there is a hidden area present and the tool supports overwriting sectors contained in a hidden area, then all sectors contained in the hidden area shall be overwritten with the specified benign data. FMP-AO-02 A hidden area may optionally be removed from the storage device.
Tester Name:	csr
Analysis host:	frank
Test host:	frank
Test date:	Mon Mar 14 12:13:26 2011
Test drive:	1C-SATA

Source Setup:	Size with DCO: 224441648 114.91 GB (10000000 sectors in DCO)
	Size with HPA: 209441648 107.23 GB (15000000 sectors in HPA)
	Initial setup size: 209441648 from total of 234441648 (with 25000000 hidden)
	IDE disk: Model (WDC WD1200JD-00GBB0) serial # (WD-WMAES2049679)
	
	Sector 0 is first sector with printable text
	============= Start text =============
	00000/000/01 000000000000
	============= End text Sector 0 =============
	1 \<new line> character inserted for readability
	
	Totals for all sectors
	summary format: \<count> \<hex value> \<(actual character if printable)> ...
	   224441648 00 109078640928 1C 224441648 20 ( )
	   448883296 2F (/) 1412016107 30 (0) 648943731 31 (1)
	   464424111 32 (2) 386665415 33 (3) 366881143 34 (4)
	   361115515 35 (5) 335339466 36 (6) 320942106 37 (7)
	   320928507 38 (8) 320460155 39 (9)
	Totals for non-ASCII sectors
	summary format: \<count> \<hex value> \<(actual character if printable)> ...
	
	114914123776 bytes, 224441648 sectors, 14 distinct values seen
	224441648 sectors have printable text

Tool Settings:	type: wipe pattern: 'b9'
Log Highlights:	======== dc3dd tool log (start) =========== dc3dd 7.0.0 started at 2011-03-15 03:36:36 -0400 compiled options: DEFAULT_HASH_MD5 (hash=md5) DEFAULT_HASH_SHA1 (hash=sha1) DEFAULT_VERBOSE_REPORTING (verb=on) command line: dc3dd wipe=/dev/sda pat=b9 log=tool-log.txt device size: 224441648 sectors (probed) sector size: 512 bytes (probed) 114914123776 bytes (107 G) copied (100%), 2533.24 s, 43 M/s input results for pattern `b9':    224441648 sectors in    2a78258b6331e8868d6e1fbd7ca00162 (md5)    adb6bad83ee5b8243781352a7f1e7f6f07251522 (sha1)  output results for device `/dev/sda': 224441648 sectors out dc3dd completed at 2011-03-15 04:18:49 -0400 ======== dc3dd tool log (end) =========== Size after tool runs: 209441648 from total of 234441648 (with 25000000 hidden)

```
                    Analysis of tool result --

                    Sector 224441648 is first sector with printable text
                    ============= Start text =============
                    13970/215/54 000224441648
                    ============= End text Sector 224441648 =============
                    1 <new line> character inserted for readability

                    Totals for all sectors
                    summary format: <count> <hex value> <(actual character if printable)> ...
                        10000000 00          4860000000 1C          10000000 20 ( )
                        20000000 2F (/)       49069416 30 (0)       29395570 31 (1)
                        33193387 32 (2)       20376376 33 (3)       24834191 34 (4)
                        14959713 35 (5)       12311991 36 (6)       11824119 37 (7)
                        11837150 38 (8)       12198087 39 (9) 114914123776 B9
                    Totals for non-ASCII sectors
                    summary format: <count> <hex value> <(actual character if printable)> ...
                    114914123776 B9

                    120034123776 bytes, 234441648 sectors, 15 distinct values seen
                    10000000 sectors have printable text


                        Runs of Sectors Unchanged or Overwritten
                    First Sector      Last Sector      State
                            0 --      224441647     Overwritten
                    224441648 --      234441647     Unchanged
```

Results:	Assertion & Expected Result	Actual Result	
	FMP-CA-01 Visible sectors overwritten	as expected	
	FMP-AO-01 Hidden sectors overwritten	DCO not overwritten	
	FMP-AO-02 Hidden area final state is	in place	
Analysis:	Expected results not achieved		

2.6.10   FMP-03-HPA

Case Summary:	FMP-03. Overwrite hidden sectors using WRITE commands.
Assertions:	FMP-CA-01 All visible sectors shall be overwritten with the specified benign data. FMP-AO-01 If there is a hidden area present and the tool supports overwriting sectors contained in a hidden area, then all sectors contained in the hidden area shall be overwritten with the specified benign data. FMP-AO-02 A hidden area may optionally be removed from the storage device.
Tester Name:	csr
Analysis host:	frank
Test host:	frank
Test date:	Tue Mar 1 14:07:24 2011
Test drive:	53-IDE
Source Setup:	Initial setup size: 297581808 from total of 312581808 (with 15000000 hidden) IDE disk: Model (WDC WD1600JB-00GVC0) serial # (WD-WMAL94865344) Sector 0 is first sector with printable text ============= Start text ============= 00000/000/01 00000000000SSSSSSSSSSSSSSSSSSSSSSSSSSSSSSSS SSSSSSSSSSSSSSSSSSSSSSSSSSSSSSSSSSSSSSSSSSSSSSSSSSSSSSSS SSSSSSSSSSSSSSSSSSSSSSSSSSSSSSSSSSSSSSSSSSSSSSSSSSSSSSSS SSSSSSSSSSSSSSSSSSSSSSSSSSSSSSSSSSSSSSSSSSSSSSSSSSSSSSSS SSSSSSSSSSSSSSSSSSSSSSSSSSSSSSSSSSSSSSSSSSSSSSSSSSSSSSSS SSSSSSSSSSSSSSSSSSSSSSSSSSSSSSSSSSSSSSSSSSSSSSSSSSSSSSSS SSSSSSSSSSSSSSSSSSSSSSSSSSSSSSSSSSSSSSSSSSSSSSSSSSSSSSSS SSSSSSSSSSSSSSSSSSSSSSSSSSSSSSSSSSSSSSSSSSSSSSSSSSSSSSSS SSSSSSSSSSSSSSSSSSSSSSSSSSSSSSS

	============= End text Sector 0 =============
	9 <new line> characters inserted for readability
	
	Totals for all sectors
	summary format: <count> <hex value> <(actual character if printable)> ...
	   312581808 00 312581808 20 ( ) 625163616 2F (/)
	  1850492169 30 (0) 906528227 31 (1) 696435016 32 (2)
	   541016511 33 (3) 522787395 34 (4) 514450557 35 (5)
	   478352540 36 (6) 458495114 37 (7) 458481159 38 (8)
	   449761088 39 (9) 151914758688 53 (S)
	Totals for non-ASCII sectors
	summary format: <count> <hex value> <(actual character if printable)> ...
	
	160041885696 bytes, 312581808 sectors, 14 distinct values seen
	312581808 sectors have printable text

Tool Settings:	type: wipe pattern: none
Log Highlights:	======== dc3dd tool log (start) =========== dc3dd 7.0.0 started at 2011-03-01 10:16:53 -0500 compiled options: DEFAULT_HASH_MD5 (hash=md5) DEFAULT_HASH_SHA1 (hash=sha1) DEFAULT_VERBOSE_REPORTING (verb=on) command line: dc3dd wipe=/dev/sda log=tool-log.txt device size: 312581808 sectors (probed) sector size: 512 bytes (probed) 160041885696 bytes (149 G) copied (100%), 3109.05 s, 49 M/s input results for pattern `00':    312581808 sectors in    26e628892c9cbb7bd4936d180f43b67d (md5)    a44050d78408a43e8dddc68ad90857686096fd76 (sha1)  output results for device `/dev/sda': 312581808 sectors out dc3dd completed at 2011-03-01 11:08:42 -0500 ======== dc3dd tool log (end) =========== Size after tool runs: 297581808 from total of 312581808 (with 15000000 hidden) Analysis of tool result -- Totals for all sectors summary format: <count> <hex value> <(actual character if printable)> ... 160041885696 00 Totals for non-ASCII sectors summary format: <count> <hex value> <(actual character if printable)> ... 160041885696 00 160041885696 bytes, 312581808 sectors, 1 distinct values seen No sectors have printable text Runs of Sectors Unchanged or Overwritten First Sector Last Sector State 0 -- 312581807 Overwritten

Results:	**Assertion & Expected Result**	**Actual Result**	
	FMP-CA-01 Visible sectors overwritten	as expected	
	FMP-AO-01 Hidden sectors overwritten	as expected	
	FMP-AO-02 Hidden area final state is	in place	

Analysis:	Expected results achieved

About the National Institute of Justice

A component of the Office of Justice Programs, NIJ is the research, development and evaluation agency of the U.S. Department of Justice. NIJ's mission is to advance scientific research, development and evaluation to enhance the administration of justice and public safety. NIJ's principal authorities are derived from the Omnibus Crime Control and Safe Streets Act of 1968, as amended (see 42 U.S.C. §§ 3721–3723).

The NIJ Director is appointed by the President and confirmed by the Senate. The Director establishes the Institute's objectives, guided by the priorities of the Office of Justice Programs, the U.S. Department of Justice, and the needs of the field. The Institute actively solicits the views of criminal justice and other professionals and researchers to inform its search for the knowledge and tools to guide policy and practice.

Strategic Goals

NIJ has seven strategic goals grouped into three categories:

Creating relevant knowledge and tools

1. Partner with state and local practitioners and policymakers to identify social science research and technology needs.
2. Create scientific, relevant, and reliable knowledge—with a particular emphasis on terrorism, violent crime, drugs and crime, cost-effectiveness, and community-based efforts—to enhance the administration of justice and public safety.
3. Develop affordable and effective tools and technologies to enhance the administration of justice and public safety.

Dissemination

4. Disseminate relevant knowledge and information to practitioners and policymakers in an understandable, timely and concise manner.
5. Act as an honest broker to identify the information, tools and technologies that respond to the needs of stakeholders.

Agency management

6. Practice fairness and openness in the research and development process.
7. Ensure professionalism, excellence, accountability, cost-effectiveness and integrity in the management and conduct of NIJ activities and programs.

Program Areas

In addressing these strategic challenges, the Institute is involved in the following program areas: crime control and prevention, including policing; drugs and crime; justice systems and offender behavior, including corrections; violence and victimization; communications and information technologies; critical incident response; investigative and forensic sciences, including DNA; less-than-lethal technologies; officer protection; education and training technologies; testing and standards; technology assistance to law enforcement and corrections agencies; field testing of promising programs; and international crime control.

In addition to sponsoring research and development and technology assistance, NIJ evaluates programs, policies, and technologies. NIJ communicates its research and evaluation findings through conferences and print and electronic media.

To find out more about the National Institute of Justice, please visit:

www.nij.gov

or contact:

National Criminal Justice
 Reference Service
P.O. Box 6000
Rockville, MD 20849–6000
800–851–3420
http://www.ncjrs.gov